INDULGENCE

chocolate

a fine selection of sweet treats

MURDOCH BOOKS

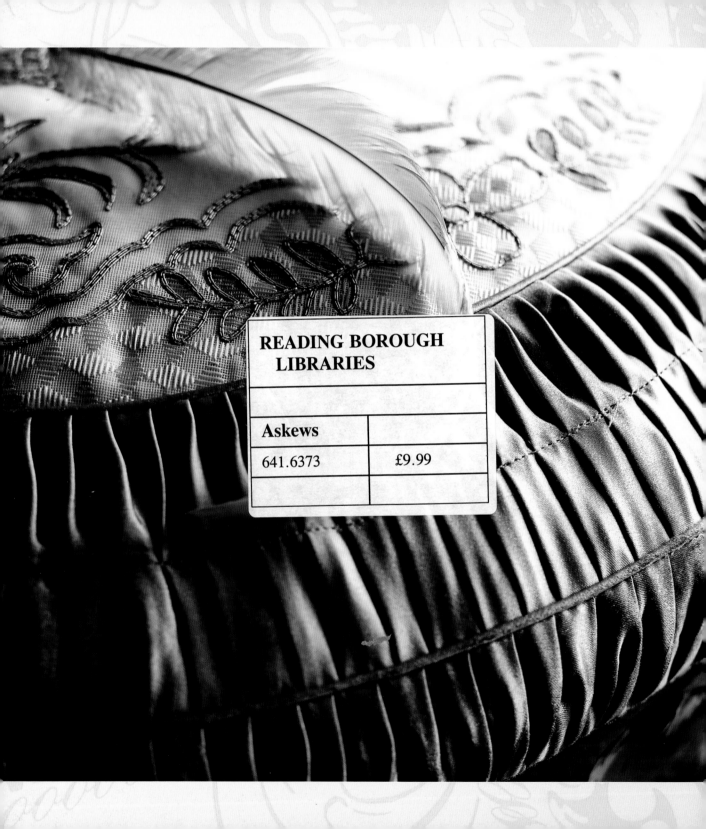

Contents

New classics

Featuring all your favourites with a delightful modern twist.

Melt-and-mix chocolate cakes

MAKES 12

150 g (5½ oz) unsalted butter, cubed
230 g (8 oz/1 cup) soft brown sugar
185 ml (6 fl oz/¾ cup) freshly made espresso coffee
2 eggs, at room temperature, lightly whisked
125 g (4½ oz/1 cup) self-raising flour
30 g (1 oz/¼ cup) plain (all-purpose) flour
60 g (2¼ oz/½ cup) unsweetened cocoa powder
¼ teaspoon bicarbonate of soda (baking soda)
icing (confectioners') sugar, sifted, for dusting

Chocolate butter cream
250 g (9 oz/2 cups) icing (confectioners') sugar, sifted
2 tablespoons unsweetened cocoa powder
60 g (2¼ oz/¼ cup) unsalted butter, softened
2 tablespoons hot water

Preheat the oven to 180°C (350°F/Gas 4). Line a 12-hole standard muffin tin with paper cases.

Combine the butter, brown sugar and coffee in a saucepan over medium heat. Stir until the butter has melted and the sugar has dissolved. Remove from the heat and cool slightly.

Whisk the eggs into the butter mixture. In a separate bowl, sift together the flours, cocoa and bicarbonate of soda. Stir half the flour mixture into the butter mixture until just combined. Add the remaining flour mixture and stir until just combined. Transfer the mixture to a jug and pour into the prepared tin. Bake for 20 minutes, or until a skewer inserted in the centre of a cake comes out clean. Allow the cakes to cool in the tin for 3 minutes, then transfer to a wire rack to cool completely.

To make the chocolate butter cream, place 125 g (4½ oz/1 cup) of the sugar in a large bowl, add the cocoa, butter and water and beat with electric beaters until smooth and creamy. Gradually add the remaining sugar and beat until the butter cream is thick.

Spread the butter cream over the cooled cakes using a spatula or flat-bladed knife.

The un-iced cakes will keep, stored in an airtight container, for up to 5 days. Iced cakes will keep in the same way for up to 2 days.

6

Homemade chocolate freckles

Line a large tray with baking paper.

Place the chocolate in a heatproof bowl over a saucepan of simmering water, ensuring the bowl doesn't touch the water. Stir until the chocolate has melted. Remove from the heat.

Working with 2 teaspoons of the chocolate at a time, shape into 12 rounds on the prepared tray 5 cm (2 inches) apart. Lightly tap the tray on the bench to spread the chocolate out to form 5 cm (2 inch) discs. Top the chocolate discs with the sprinkles of your choice. Stand at room temperature for 30 minutes, or until set.

The chocolate freckles will keep, stored in an airtight container in a cool place, for up to 2 weeks.

MAKES 12

150 g (5½ oz) milk chocolate melts (buttons)
ready-made sprinkles of your choice (such as hundreds and thousands, silver or mixed cachous and/or coloured sprinkles)

Chocolate, almond and pear puddings

MAKES 8

115 g (4 oz/⅓ cup) golden syrup (light treacle)
8 tinned pear halves in natural juice, drained
60 g (2¼ oz/½ cup) plain (all-purpose) flour
30 g (1 oz/¼ cup) unsweetened cocoa powder
2 teaspoons baking powder
1 teaspoon ground allspice (optional)
55 g (2 oz/½ cup) ground almonds
3 eggs, at room temperature
165 g (5¾ oz/¾ cup) soft brown sugar
60 ml (2 fl oz/¼ cup) milk
115 g (4 oz/⅓ cup) golden syrup (light treacle),
extra, warmed slightly
vanilla ice cream or thick (double/heavy) cream

Preheat the oven to 180°C (350°F/Gas 4). Grease eight holes of two non-stick six-hole giant muffin tins and line the bases with baking paper.

Spoon the golden syrup into the prepared tins to cover the bases. Place a pear half, cut side down, in each.

Sift together the flour, cocoa, baking powder and allspice, if using, into a medium-sized bowl, then stir in the ground almonds.

Beat the eggs and sugar in a large bowl using electric beaters until pale and creamy. Slowly pour in the milk, add the flour mixture and use a large metal spoon or spatula to fold in until just combined.

Spoon the pudding mixture over the pears. Bake for 25 minutes, or until cooked when a skewer inserted into the centre of a pudding comes out clean. Allow to cool in the tins for 3 minutes, then turn out onto a wire rack. Immediately remove the paper rounds and transfer the puddings to serving plates. Drizzle with the extra golden syrup and serve accompanied by ice cream or cream.

Halva with chocolate and star anise syrup

MAKES 16

125 g (4½ oz/½ cup) unsalted butter, softened
115 g (4 oz/½ cup) caster (superfine) sugar
finely grated zest of 1 orange
175 g (6 oz/1 cup) fine semolina
2 teaspoons baking powder
3 eggs, at room temperature
110 g (3¾ oz/1 cup) ground hazelnuts
120 g (4¼ oz) hazelnuts, toasted, skinned and roughly chopped
thick (double/heavy) cream

Chocolate and star anise syrup
345 g (12 oz/1½ cups) caster (superfine) sugar
2 tablespoons unsweetened cocoa powder, sifted
500 ml (17 fl oz/2 cups) water
3 star anise

Preheat the oven to 180°C (350°F/Gas 4). Grease a 20 cm (8 inch) square cake tin and line the base with baking paper.

Cream the butter, sugar and orange zest in a medium-sized bowl using electric beaters until pale and fluffy. Sift in the semolina and baking powder, add the eggs and ground hazelnuts and beat until well combined. Spoon into the prepared tin and smooth the surface with the back of a spoon. Bake for 30 minutes, or until a skewer inserted in the centre comes out clean. Allow to cool in the tin on a wire rack.

Meanwhile, to make the chocolate and star anise syrup, combine the sugar and cocoa in a saucepan and gradually stir in the water. Add the star anise and stir over medium heat until the sugar has dissolved. Bring to the boil and simmer, without stirring, for 10 minutes, or until slightly reduced and syrupy. Pour half the syrup over the cooled halva in the tin. Set aside for 20 minutes, or until the syrup has been absorbed.

Boil the remaining syrup over medium heat for
10 minutes, or until reduced to 250 ml (9 fl oz/1 cup).

Run a flat-bladed knife around the halva and turn out
onto a cutting board. Cut into four squares and then
cut each square into four triangles. Pour a little of the
remaining syrup over the halva, sprinkle on the
hazelnuts and serve accompanied by the cream.

The halva will keep, stored in an airtight container
in the refrigerator, for up to 4 days.

Chocolate and cinnamon ice-cream sandwiches

MAKES 10

10 small scoops chocolate ice cream

Cinnamon biscuits (cookies)
115 g (4 oz/⅓ cup) golden syrup (light treacle)
80 g (2¾ oz/⅓ cup) caster (superfine) sugar
60 g (2¼ oz/¼ cup) butter, cubed
155 g (5½ oz/1¼ cups) plain (all-purpose) flour
½ teaspoon baking powder
2 teaspoons ground cinnamon
1½ tablespoons raw (demerara) sugar

Preheat the oven to 200°C (400°F/Gas 6). Line two baking trays with baking paper.

To make the cinnamon biscuits, combine the golden syrup, caster sugar and butter in a saucepan and stir over low heat until the butter has melted and the sugar has dissolved. Pour into a heatproof bowl and set aside to cool for 10 minutes. Sift in the flour, baking powder and cinnamon and, using a wooden spoon, stir to form a firm dough. Divide the dough in half. Roll out one portion on a lightly floured work surface until 5 mm (¼ inch) thick. Use a 6 cm (2½ inch) fluted round cookie cutter or an 8 cm (3¼ inch) flower-shaped cutter to cut out 10 shapes, re-rolling any off-cuts. Place on a prepared tray about 2 cm (¾ inch) apart and sprinkle on half the raw sugar. Repeat with the remaining dough and sugar. Transfer to the refrigerator for 20 minutes. Bake for 8–10 minutes, or until lightly golden around the edges. Allow to cool on the trays.

To assemble, line a tray with baking paper and transfer to the freezer. Place a scoop of ice cream on the base of a biscuit, top with a second biscuit, sugar side up, and press to flatten slightly. Transfer to the prepared tray. Repeat with the remaining biscuits and ice cream. Freeze for 2 hours, or until the ice cream is firm.

These ice-cream sandwiches will keep, individually covered with plastic wrap and stored in an airtight container in the freezer, for up to 1 week.

Walnut and fig hedgehog bars

MAKES 21

Line the base and sides of an 18 cm (7 inch) square cake tin with baking paper, extending the paper over two opposite sides for easy removal later.

Combine the biscuits, figs and walnuts in a medium-sized bowl and set aside.

Place the chocolate, butter and honey in a small saucepan and stir over low heat until the chocolate and butter have melted. Add to the biscuit mixture and stir with a wooden spoon to combine. Spoon into the prepared tin and tap gently on the bench to settle the mixture. Cover with plastic wrap and refrigerate for 1 hour, or until firm. Remove from the tin and cut into 2.5 x 6 cm (1 x 2½ inch) bars. To serve, dust with the sugar or cocoa, if desired.

These bars will keep, stored in an airtight container in the refrigerator, for up to 1 month.

100 g (3½ oz) digestive or shredded
   wheatmeal biscuits (cookies), broken into
   2 cm (¾ inch) pieces
125 g (4½ oz/⅔ cup) chopped dried figs
50 g (1¾ oz/½ cup) walnut halves,
   roughly chopped
300 g (10½ oz) dark chocolate (54 per cent cocoa
   solids), chopped
60 g (2¼ oz/¼ cup) unsalted butter, chopped
90 g (3¼ oz/¼ cup) honey
icing (confectioners') sugar or sweetened cocoa
   powder, sifted, for dusting (optional)

Iced chocolate

SERVES 4

125 g (4½ oz) dark chocolate (54 per cent cocoa
solids), chopped
160 ml (5¼ fl oz) cream (whipping)
750 ml (26 fl oz/3 cups) milk
8 small or 4 generous scoops chocolate ice cream
shaved dark chocolate (54 per cent cocoa solids),
to sprinkle

Combine the chopped chocolate and cream in a small saucepan over low heat. Stir until the chocolate has melted. Transfer the chocolate sauce to a jug and set aside to cool.

Pour the chocolate mixture down the side of four tall 250 ml (9 fl oz/1 cup) glasses to coat the inside. Divide the milk and ice cream among the glasses, sprinkle on the shaved chocolate and serve immediately.

The chocolate sauce will keep, stored in an airtight container in the refrigerator, for up to 5 days. Warm it slightly to a pouring consistency before using.

Rich hot chocolate

SERVES 4

125 ml (4 fl oz/½ cup) thickened
(whipping) cream
75 g (2¾ oz) dark chocolate (54 per cent cocoa
solids), finely chopped
375 ml (13 fl oz/1½ cups) milk
sweetened cocoa powder, sifted, for dusting

Beat the cream in a medium-sized bowl using electric beaters until soft peaks form. Set aside.

Place the chocolate in a heatproof jug.

Heat the milk in a small saucepan over medium heat until almost simmering. Pour over the chocolate. Stand for 1 minute and stir until the chocolate has melted. Pour immediately into four small glasses or cups. Top with a generous dollop of whipped cream and dust with the cocoa.

Chocolate, blackberry and coconut slice

MAKES 28

180 g (6¼ oz/2 cups) desiccated coconut
250 g (9 oz/2 cups) plain (all-purpose)
 flour, sifted
165 g (5¾ oz/¾ cup) soft brown sugar
200 g (7 oz) dark chocolate (54 per cent cocoa
 solids), chopped
100 g (3½ oz) unsalted butter, chopped
2 eggs, at room temperature, lightly whisked
160 g (5¾ oz/½ cup) blackberry jam
icing (confectioners') sugar, sifted, for dusting

Preheat the oven to 170°C (325°F/Gas 3). Line the base and sides of an 18 x 28 cm (7 x 11¼ inch) baking tin with baking paper, extending the paper over two long sides for easy removal later.

Combine the coconut, flour and brown sugar in a large bowl and set aside.

Place the chocolate and butter in a small saucepan and stir over low heat until the chocolate and butter have melted. Add to the coconut mixture with the eggs and stir with a wooden spoon until combined.

Spoon half the chocolate mixture into the prepared tin and press down firmly with the back of a spoon. Spread the jam over the top, then add the remaining chocolate mixture, pressing with the back of the spoon to smooth the surface.

Bake for 50 minutes, or until a skewer inserted in the centre of the slice comes out clean. Allow to cool in the tin for 10 minutes, then transfer to a wire rack to cool completely. Cut into 4 x 4.5 cm (1½ x 1¾ inch) pieces and serve dusted with the icing sugar.

This slice will keep, stored in an airtight container, for up to 5 days.

Real chocolate
crackles

MAKES 36

75 g (2¾ oz/2½ cups) puffed rice cereal
90 g (3¼ oz/1 cup) desiccated coconut
250 g (9 oz) dark chocolate (54 per cent cocoa
solids), chopped
icing (confectioners') sugar, sifted,
for dusting (optional)

Line three 12-hole mini muffin tins with paper cases.

Combine the puffed rice and coconut in a large bowl. Place the chocolate in a heatproof bowl over a saucepan of simmering water, ensuring the bowl doesn't touch the water. Stir until the chocolate has melted. Remove from the heat.

Add the melted chocolate to the puffed rice mixture and, using a wooden spoon, stir gently until evenly combined. Spoon the mixture into the paper cases. Place in the refrigerator for 1 hour, or until set. Dust with the icing sugar if desired.

The chocolate crackles will keep, stored in an airtight container in the refrigerator, for up to 2 weeks.

TIP: You can also make delicate, bite-sized chocolate crackles to serve with coffee. Use 72 confectionery chocolate cases instead of the mini muffin paper cases.

Chocolate mousse ice cream

Place the chocolate in a heatproof bowl over a saucepan of simmering water, ensuring the bowl doesn't touch the water. Stir until the chocolate has melted. Set aside to cool to lukewarm.

Beat the egg yolks into the melted chocolate using a wooden spoon and stir in the brandy, if using.

Beat the egg whites in a medium-sized bowl using electric beaters until soft peaks form. Add the sugar and beat until the sugar has dissolved and the mixture is thick and glossy. Use a large metal spoon to fold the egg white mixture into the cooled chocolate mixture in two batches.

Whip the cream in a medium-sized bowl using electric beaters until soft peaks form, then fold into the chocolate mixture. Pour the mixture into a 1 litre (35 fl oz/4 cup) airtight container, seal and freeze for 6 hours, or until frozen.

Serve small scoops in the ice-cream cones, if using, or in small bowls.

This ice cream will keep, stored in an airtight container in the freezer, for up to 2 weeks.

SERVES 12

165 g (5¾ oz) dark chocolate (54 per cent cocoa solids), chopped
2 eggs, at room temperature, separated
1 tablespoon brandy (optional)
2 tablespoons caster (superfine) sugar
125 ml (4 fl oz/½ cup) whipping cream
12 mini ice-cream cones (optional)

Mini chocolate and banana loaves

MAKES 6

60 g (2¼ oz/¼ cup) unsalted butter, softened
115 g (4 oz/½ cup) soft brown sugar
1 egg, at room temperature
120 g (4¼ oz/½ cup) mashed banana
100 g (3½ oz) dark chocolate, chopped
125 g (4½ oz/1 cup) plain (all-purpose) flour
1½ teaspoons ground cinnamon
½ teaspoon bicarbonate of soda (baking soda)
60 ml (2 fl oz/¼ cup) buttermilk
icing (confectioners') sugar, sifted, for dusting (optional)

Preheat the oven to 190°C (375°F/Gas 5). Grease six 5 x 8 x 4 cm (2 x 3¼ x 1½ inch) loaf (bar) tins and line the bases with baking paper.

Cream the butter and brown sugar in a medium-sized bowl using electric beaters until pale and fluffy. Add the egg and beat until well combined. Stir in the banana and chocolate. In a separate bowl, sift together the flour, cinnamon and bicarbonate of soda. Fold half of the flour mixture into the chocolate mixture. Fold in the buttermilk, then add the remaining flour mixture and stir until just combined.

Spoon into the prepared tins and smooth the surfaces with the back of a spoon. Bake for 25–30 minutes, or until a skewer inserted in the centre of a loaf comes out clean. Allow to stand in the tins for 5 minutes, then turn out onto a wire rack to cool completely. Serve dusted with the icing sugar, if desired.

These loaves will keep, stored in an airtight container, for up to 3 days. To freeze, cover individually with plastic wrap and place in an airtight container or a freezer bag. Seal and freeze for up to 3 months. Thaw at room temperature.

TIP: For 120 g (4¼ oz/½ cup) mashed banana you will need one 200 g (7 oz) very ripe banana.

Chocolate orange fudge

Line the base and sides of an 18 cm (7 inch) square cake tin with baking paper, extending the paper over two opposite sides for easy removal later.

Place the condensed milk and butter in a heavy-based saucepan and cook over low heat, stirring occasionally, until the butter has melted. Bring just to a simmer, stirring frequently. Remove from the heat and set aside for 5 minutes to cool slightly. Add both types of the chocolate and stir until the chocolate has melted.

Working quickly, pour the fudge mixture into the prepared tin and use the back of a metal spoon to smooth the surface. Place in the refrigerator for 4 hours, or until firm.

Remove the fudge from the tin and cut into 3 cm (1¼ inch) squares.

This fudge will keep, with the layers separated by baking paper, stored in an airtight container in the refrigerator, for up to 1 month.

TIP: Don't use orange-flavoured chocolate with a soft or liquid centre.

MAKES 36

395 g (13¾ oz) tin sweetened condensed milk
50 g (1¾ oz) unsalted butter, cubed
200 g (7 oz) orange-flavoured dark chocolate, finely chopped
200 g (7 oz) dark chocolate (54 per cent cocoa solids), finely chopped

Chocolate beetroot cakes

MAKES 12

canola oil spray, to grease
125 g (4½ oz/1 cup) plain (all-purpose) flour
40 g (1½ oz/⅓ cup) unsweetened cocoa powder
1½ teaspoons bicarbonate of soda (baking soda)
½ teaspoon baking powder
1 teaspoon mixed (pumpkin pie) spice (optional)
230 g (8 oz/1 cup) soft brown sugar
75 g (2¾ oz/¾ cup) walnut halves, chopped
170 ml (5½ fl oz/⅔ cup) canola or vegetable oil
2 eggs, at room temperature
225 g (8 oz/1½ cups) coarsely grated beetroot
unsweetened cocoa powder, sifted, for dusting
thick (double/heavy) cream or
vanilla ice cream (optional)

Preheat the oven to 180°C (350°F/Gas 4). Spray twelve 125 ml (4 fl oz/½ cup) fluted ring tins with the oil and place on a baking tray.

Sift the flour, cocoa, bicarbonate of soda, baking powder and mixed spice, if using, into a large bowl. Stir in the sugar and walnuts and make a well in the centre.

Whisk the oil and eggs in a medium-sized bowl until well combined, then stir in the beetroot. Fold into the flour mixture using a large metal spoon. Spoon into the prepared tins and smooth the surfaces with the back of a spoon. Bake for 20 minutes, or until a skewer inserted in the centre of a cake comes out clean. Allow to stand in the tins for 5 minutes, then turn out onto a wire rack to cool completely.

Dust with cocoa and serve with the cream or ice cream, if desired.

These cakes will keep, stored in an airtight container, for up to 3 days.

Chocolate and hazelnut self-saucing puddings

Preheat the oven to 170°C (325°F/Gas 3). Grease six 185 ml (6 fl oz/¾ cup) ovenproof dishes and place on a baking tray.

Sift together the flour and cocoa into a medium-sized bowl. Stir in the brown sugar and hazelnuts. Place the milk, egg and butter in a jug or bowl and, using a fork, whisk until well combined. Add to the cocoa mixture and stir with a wooden spoon until just combined. Pour into the prepared dishes and smooth the surfaces with the back of a spoon.

To make the sauce, combine the sugar and cocoa in a small bowl and sprinkle evenly over the pudding mixture. Pour the boiling water over the cocoa and sugar mixture.

Bake for 25 minutes, or until the top of each pudding is firm to touch. Stand for 5 minutes. Serve dusted with the icing sugar.

TIPS: Smoothing the surface of the puddings before adding the sauce ingredients helps them to rise evenly. If you are using shallow ovenproof dishes, reduce the cooking time to 20 minutes.

MAKES 6

125 g (4½ oz/1 cup) self-raising flour
2½ tablespoons unsweetened cocoa powder
80 g (2¾ oz/⅓ cup) soft brown sugar
60 g (2¼ oz) hazelnuts, toasted, skinned and roughly chopped
160 ml (5¼ fl oz) milk
1 egg
60 g (2¼ oz/¼ cup) butter, melted and cooled
icing (confectioners') sugar, sifted, for dusting

Sauce
115 g (4 oz/½ cup) soft brown sugar
30 g (1 oz/¼ cup) unsweetened cocoa powder, sifted
310 ml (10¾ fl oz/1¼ cups) boiling water

Chocolate meringues

MAKES ABOUT 24

2 egg whites, at room temperature
pinch of salt
115 g (4 oz/½ cup) caster (superfine) sugar
75 g (2¾ oz) dark chocolate (70 per cent cocoa
solids), coarsely grated
unsweetened cocoa powder, sifted, for dusting
(optional)

Preheat the oven to 120°C (235°F/Gas ½). Line two baking trays with baking paper.

Beat the egg whites and salt in a medium-sized bowl using electric beaters until soft peaks form. Add the sugar, a spoonful at a time, and beat until the sugar has dissolved, the mixture is thick and glossy and a long trailing peak forms when the beater is lifted. Use a large metal spoon or spatula to fold in the chocolate.

Spoon large teaspoonfuls of the mixture onto the prepared trays about 2 cm (¾ inch) apart. Dust with the cocoa, if desired.

Place the meringues in the oven and immediately reduce the temperature to 100°C (200°F/Gas ½). Bake for 1½ hours, or until the meringues are crisp and sound hollow when tapped on the base. Turn off the oven and leave the door slightly ajar, allowing the meringues to cool slowly.

These meringues will keep, stored in an airtight container, for up to 1 week.

Chocolate clusters

Line a tray with baking paper.

Place the chocolate in a heatproof bowl over a saucepan of simmering water, ensuring the bowl doesn't touch the water. Stir until the chocolate has melted. Remove from the heat.

Stir the coconut, almonds and figs into the chocolate until evenly combined. Shape teaspoons of the mixture into small clusters and place on the prepared tray. Stand at room temperature for 4–6 hours, or until the chocolate has set.

These clusters will keep, stored in an airtight container in a cool place, for up to 1 week.

TIPS: To lightly toast the coconut and almonds, spread separately on two baking trays. Bake, shaking the trays once during cooking, in a preheated 180°C (350°F/Gas 4) oven for 3 minutes for the coconut and 6 minutes for the almonds, or until each is lightly toasted. Allow to cool on the trays.
You can use dark chocolate (54 per cent cocoa solids) in place of the milk chocolate, if you wish.
The time that the chocolate clusters take to set depends on the weather: in warmer weather you may have to leave them to set overnight.

MAKES ABOUT 15

200 g (7 oz) milk chocolate, chopped
30 g (1 oz/½ cup) flaked coconut, lightly toasted
30 g (1 oz/¼ cup) slivered almonds, lightly toasted
45 g (1¾ oz/¼ cup) chopped dried figs

Lamington wedges

MAKES 8

1 x 17 cm (6½ inch) round ready-made
sponge cake
110 g (3¾ oz/2 cups) flaked coconut or
180 g (6¼ oz/3 cups) shredded coconut

Chocolate icing (frosting)
250 g (9 oz/2 cups) icing (confectioners') sugar
40 g (1½ oz/⅓ cup) unsweetened cocoa powder
125 ml (4 fl oz/½ cup) boiling water
30 g (1 oz) unsalted butter, cubed
1 teaspoon natural vanilla extract

Trim the top and side of the sponge cake using a
serrated knife and cut the cake into eight wedges.
Spread the coconut on a plate.

To make the chocolate icing, sift the sugar and cocoa
into a heatproof bowl and make a well in the centre. In
a separate bowl, combine the boiling water, butter and
vanilla and stir until the butter has melted. Add to the
sugar mixture and stir until smooth.

Use two forks to carefully coat a cake wedge in the
warm icing, allowing any excess icing to drip off.
Roll the cake in the coconut and place on a wire rack.
Repeat with the remaining cake wedges, icing and
coconut. Allow to stand for 1 hour, or until the
icing has set.

These lamingtons will keep, stored in an airtight
container, for up to 3 days.

TIP: If the chocolate icing begins to cool and thicken
too much while you are coating the cake wedges, place
the bowl over a saucepan of simmering water and stir
until it thins again.

Milk chocolate and cashew truffles

MAKES ABOUT 18

150 g (5½ oz) milk chocolate, chopped
60 ml (2 fl oz/¼ cup) cream (whipping)
1 tablespoon Kahlua or Tia Maria
60 g (2¼ oz) unsalted cashew nuts, lightly
toasted and finely chopped

Place the chocolate and cream in a heatproof bowl over a saucepan of simmering water, ensuring the bowl doesn't touch the water. Stir until the chocolate has melted. Remove from the heat and stir in the liqueur. Cover with plastic wrap and transfer to the refrigerator for 1–2 hours, stirring occasionally, or until the mixture is firm enough to roll into balls.

Spread the cashew nuts on a plate. Roll small teaspoons of the chocolate mixture into balls, then roll in the cashew nuts to coat. Place the finished truffles in paper cases, if desired, transfer to a plate and return to the refrigerator for at least 1 hour before serving.

These truffles will keep, stored in an airtight container in the refrigerator, for up to 2 weeks.

TIP: Toast the cashews in a preheated 180°C (350°F/Gas 4) oven for 8–10 minutes, or until golden and aromatic. Cool on the tray, then chop.

Chocolate and pecan honey wafers

Preheat the oven to 160°C (315°F/Gas 2–3). Line two baking trays with baking paper.

Combine the flour, sugar, honey, butter and egg white in the bowl of a food processor and process until just combined. Divide the mixture between the baking trays and spread with the back of a spoon to form two thin 20 x 25 cm (8 x 10 inch) rectangles of equal thickness. Sprinkle evenly with the chocolate and pecans.

Bake, swapping the trays halfway through cooking, for 24–28 minutes, or until dark golden. Allow to cool on the trays.

Break into pieces roughly 5 cm (2 inch) and serve.

These wafers will keep, stored in an airtight container, for up to 1 week.

MAKES ABOUT 25

35 g (1¼ oz) plain (all-purpose) flour
25 g (1 oz) caster (superfine) sugar
85 g (3 oz) honey (such as iron bark or blue gum), warmed slightly
65 g (2½ oz) unsalted butter, melted and cooled
1 egg white
70 g (2½ oz) dark chocolate, roughly chopped
70 g (2½ oz) pecans, roughly chopped

The high life

Feed your chocolate addiction with this delectable array of elegant treats.

Chocolate and pistachio macaroons

MAKES ABOUT 50

120 g (4¼ oz) pistachio nuts
155 g (5½ oz/1¼ cups) icing (confectioners')
sugar, sifted, plus extra, for dusting (optional)
3 egg whites, at room temperature
2 tablespoons caster (superfine) sugar
7 drops green food colouring, or as desired

Chocolate ganache
200 g (7 oz) dark chocolate (54 per cent cocoa
solids), finely chopped
100 ml (3½ fl oz) cream

Preheat the oven to 150°C (300°F/Gas 2). Line two baking trays with baking paper.

Place the pistachio nuts in the bowl of a food processor and process until finely ground. Transfer to a medium-sized bowl, add the icing sugar, mix well and set aside.

Beat the egg whites in a large bowl using electric beaters until soft peaks form. Add the caster sugar, a spoonful at a time, and beat until the sugar has dissolved and the mixture is thick and glossy. Beat in the food colouring, then use a large metal spoon or spatula to gently fold in the pistachio mixture.

Spoon the macaroon mixture into a piping (icing) bag fitted with a 1 cm (½ inch) plain nozzle. Pipe 3 cm (1¼ inch) rounds, about 2 cm (¾ inch) apart, onto the prepared trays. Stand at room temperature for 30 minutes. Bake, swapping the trays halfway through cooking, for 15 minutes, or until the macaroons are crisp on the outside. Turn off the oven and leave the door slightly ajar, allowing the macaroons to cool slowly.

Meanwhile, to make the chocolate ganache, combine the chocolate and cream in a heatproof bowl over a saucepan of simmering water, ensuring the bowl doesn't touch the water. Stir until the chocolate has melted. Remove from the heat. Cover with plastic wrap and refrigerate, stirring occasionally, for 30 minutes, or until the ganache is a spreadable consistency.

Spread the base of half the macaroons with the chocolate ganache and sandwich together with the remaining macaroons. Dust with the extra icing sugar, if using, and serve.

Unfilled macaroons will keep, stored in an airtight container, for up to 1 week. Filled macaroons will keep, stored in an airtight container, for up to 3 days.

Chocolate peppermint squares

300 g (10½ oz) dark chocolate (54 per cent cocoa solids), chopped

Biscuits (cookies)
100 g (3½ oz) unsalted butter, cubed
115 g (4 oz/½ cup) caster (superfine) sugar
1 egg yolk
155 g (5½ oz/1¼ cups) plain (all-purpose) flour

Peppermint filling
125 g (4½ oz/1 cup) icing (confectioners') sugar
1 tablespoon boiling water
½ teaspoon peppermint essence

Preheat the oven to 180°C (350°F/Gas 4). Line two baking trays with baking paper.

To make the biscuits, place the butter, sugar and egg yolk in the bowl of a food processor and process until well combined. Add the flour and pulse until just combined. Turn out onto a lightly floured work surface and knead gently for 1–2 minutes, or until the dough just comes together. Divide the dough in half. Roll out each portion between two pieces of baking paper to 3 mm (⅛ inch) thick. Refrigerate for 30 minutes, then, using a ruler, cut the dough into 3 cm (1¼ inch) squares, re-rolling the scraps and cutting out more squares. Place the squares, about 2 cm (¾ inch) apart, on the prepared trays. Transfer to the refrigerator for 10 minutes. Bake, swapping the trays halfway through cooking, for 12 minutes, or until lightly golden. Allow the squares to cool on the trays.

To make the peppermint filling, sift the sugar into a small bowl. Add the water and peppermint essence and stir until smooth.

Sandwich the squares together with the peppermint filling. Transfer to a tray lined with baking paper and refrigerate for 20 minutes.

Meanwhile, place the chocolate in a heatproof bowl over a saucepan of simmering water, ensuring the bowl doesn't touch the water. Stir until the chocolate has melted. Remove from the heat. Using two forks, dip each sandwiched biscuit into the chocolate to coat, allowing the excess to drip off. Return to the tray and stand in a cool place until the chocolate has set.

These biscuits will keep, stored in an airtight container in a cool place, for up to 1 week.

TIP: The time the chocolate takes to set depends on the weather: the cooler the weather, the less time it will take.

Chocolate and ricotta fritters

Combine the ricotta, egg, egg yolk, sugar and brandy in a medium-sized bowl and beat with a wooden spoon until well combined (the ricotta will still be a little lumpy). Mix in the flour, then stir in the chocolate. Cover and set aside for 15 minutes.

Preheat the oven to 120°C (235°F/Gas ½). Line a baking tray with paper towel and place a wire rack on top.

Heat the oil in a large heavy-based saucepan over medium heat to 180°C (350°F), or until a cube of bread dropped into the oil browns in 15 seconds. Add teaspoons of the ricotta mixture, in batches of about 10 at a time, to the hot oil. Cook, turning occasionally, for 3–4 minutes, or until golden and cooked through. Use a slotted spoon to transfer the fritters from the oil to the prepared rack. Place in the oven to keep warm. Repeat with the remaining ricotta mixture.

When the final batch has been cooked, drain for 2 minutes on the wire rack. Combine the extra sugar and the cinnamon in a shallow bowl. Toss the fritters, in batches, in the cinnamon sugar to coat. Place on a serving plate and sprinkle with any remaining cinnamon sugar. Serve immediately.

MAKES ABOUT 30

250 g (9 oz) fresh ricotta cheese, drained overnight

1 egg

1 egg yolk

2 tablespoons caster (superfine) sugar

1 tablespoon brandy

40 g (1½ oz/⅓ cup) self-raising flour, sifted

75 g (2¾ oz) dark chocolate (54 per cent cocoa solids), finely chopped

1 litre (35 fl oz/4 cups) vegetable oil, for deep frying

55 g (2 oz/¼ cup) caster (superfine) sugar, extra

½ teaspoon ground cinnamon

Cinnamon chocolate kisses

MAKES ABOUT 50

250 g (9 oz/1 cup) unsalted butter, softened
85 g (3 oz/⅔ cup) icing (confectioners') sugar
155 g (5½ oz/1¼ cups) plain (all-purpose) flour
40 g (1½ oz/⅓ cup) cornflour (cornstarch)
30 g (1 oz/¼ cup) unsweetened cocoa powder
2½ teaspoons ground cinnamon

Chocolate ganache
80 ml (2½ fl oz/⅓ cup) cream (whipping)
120 g (4¼ oz) dark chocolate (54 per cent cocoa solids), finely chopped

Preheat the oven to 160°C (315°F/Gas 2–3). Line two baking trays with baking paper.

Cream the butter and sugar in a medium-sized bowl using electric beaters until pale and fluffy. Sift in the flour, cornflour, cocoa and cinnamon and beat until just combined. Spoon the mixture into a piping (icing) bag fitted with a 1 cm (½ inch) star nozzle. Pipe 3 cm (1¼ inch) stars, about 2 cm (¾ inch) apart, onto the prepared trays. Place in the refrigerator for 20 minutes. Bake, swapping the trays halfway through cooking, for 20 minutes, or until just cooked through. Allow the biscuits to cool on the trays.

Meanwhile, to make the chocolate ganache, heat the cream in a small saucepan until almost simmering. Place the chocolate in a heatproof bowl and pour on the hot cream. Stand for 1 minute, then stir until the chocolate has melted. Cover with plastic wrap and place in the refrigerator, stirring occasionally, for 30 minutes, or until the ganache is a thick, spreadable consistency.

Spread the base of half the biscuits with chocolate ganache and sandwich together with the remaining biscuits.

These kisses will keep, stored in an airtight container, for up to 5 days.

TIP: These cinnamon chocolate kisses are also delicious unfilled and dusted with icing (confectioners') sugar.

Chocolate butterfly cakes

Preheat the oven to 190°C (375°F/Gas 5). Grease 18 holes of two 12-hole non-stick mini muffin tins.

Cream the butter, sugar and vanilla in a medium-sized bowl using electric beaters until pale and fluffy. Add the egg and beat well. In a separate bowl, sift together the flour and cocoa. Add half the flour mixture to the butter mixture and beat until just combined. Add the milk and beat until just combined. Add the remaining flour mixture and beat until just combined.

Spoon the mixture into the prepared tins. Bake for 8–10 minutes, or until cooked when a skewer inserted in the centre of a cake comes out clean. Allow to stand in the tins for 2 minutes, then transfer to a wire rack to cool completely.

Cut a shallow cone-shaped piece from the top of a cooled cake. Cut the piece of cake in half to form two wedges. Fill the hollow in the centre of the cake with a little of the cream and then add a little of the raspberry jam. Lightly press the two cake wedges into the jam to form the butterfly wings. Repeat with the remaining cakes, cream and jam. Dust with the icing sugar and serve.

These butterfly cakes are best eaten the day they are made.

TIP: You can use mascarpone cheese in place of the cream.

MAKES 18

60 g (2¼ oz/¼ cup) unsalted butter, softened
80 g (2¾ oz/⅓ cup) soft brown sugar
½ teaspoon natural vanilla extract
1 egg, at room temperature
60 g (2¼ oz/½ cup) self-raising flour
30 g (1 oz/¼ cup) unsweetened cocoa powder
2 tablespoons milk
50 g (1¾ oz/¼ cup) thick (double/heavy) cream
80 g (2¾ oz/¼ cup) raspberry jam
icing (confectioners') sugar, sifted, for dusting

White chocolate and almond cakes

MAKES 12

125 g (4½ oz) white chocolate, chopped
80 g (2¾ oz) unsalted butter, cubed
100 ml (3½ fl oz) milk
115 g (4 oz/½ cup) caster (superfine) sugar
1 egg, at room temperature
90 g (3¼ oz/¾ cup) self-raising flour, sifted
55 g (2 oz/½ cup) ground almonds
12 raspberries, to decorate

White chocolate ganache
400 g (14 oz) white chocolate, finely chopped
170 ml (5½ fl oz/⅔ cup) cream (whipping)

Preheat the oven to 190°C (375°F/Gas 5). Line a 12-hole standard muffin tin with paper cases.

Combine the chocolate, butter and milk in a small saucepan over low heat and stir until the chocolate and butter have melted. Remove from the heat, transfer to a large bowl and set aside for 15 minutes, or until lukewarm.

Whisk the caster sugar and egg into the chocolate mixture. Place the flour and ground almonds in a bowl, mix well and stir into the chocolate mixture until just combined. Spoon into the prepared tin. Bake for 18 minutes, or until a skewer inserted in the centre of a cake comes out clean. Allow to stand in the tin for 5 minutes, then transfer the cakes to a wire rack and let them cool completely.

To make the white chocolate ganache, place the chocolate in a heatproof bowl. Heat the cream in a small saucepan until almost simmering. Pour onto the chocolate, set aside for 1 minute, then stir until smooth. Cover with plastic wrap and place in the refrigerator, stirring occasionally, for 30 minutes, or until a thick, spreadable consistency.

Spread the top of the cooled cakes with the ganache and top each with a raspberry.

The iced cakes will keep, stored in an airtight container in a cool place, for up to 2 days.

Chocolate oranges

Preheat the oven to 120°C (235°F/Gas ½). Line a wire rack with baking paper and place over a baking tray.

Spread the orange slices on the prepared rack and bake, turning halfway through cooking, for 2½ hours, or until dried but not coloured. Turn off the oven and allow the oranges to cool in the oven.

Place the chocolate in a heatproof bowl over a saucepan of simmering water, ensuring the bowl doesn't touch the water. Stir until the chocolate has melted. Remove from the heat.

Line a tray with baking paper. Dip half of each orange slice into the chocolate, tapping gently on the side of the bowl to remove any excess. Place on the prepared tray and stand in a cool place until the chocolate has set.

The dried orange slices (without the chocolate) will keep, stored in an airtight container, for up to 1 week. Once dipped in the chocolate they will keep for 1 day.

TIP: The time that the chocolate takes to set depends on the weather: the cooler the weather, the less time it takes.

MAKES 40

2 medium valencia oranges, ends trimmed, cut into 5 mm (¼ inch) thick slices
100 g (3½ oz) dark chocolate (54 per cent cocoa solids), chopped

The high life

Chocolate, Marsala and honey sorbet

SERVES 8

30 g (1 oz/¼ cup) unsweetened cocoa
powder, sifted
55 g (2 oz/¼ cup) caster (superfine) sugar
625 ml (21½ fl oz/2½ cups) water
175 g (6 oz/½ cup) honey
2 tablespoons dry Marsala
300 ml (10½ fl oz) whipping (cream),
lightly whipped

Combine the cocoa and sugar in a saucepan and gradually whisk in the water. Add the honey and stir over medium heat until the sugar and honey have dissolved. Bring just to the boil, remove from the heat, stir in the Marsala and set it aside. Allow it to cool to room temperature.

Pour into a 1 litre (35 fl oz/4 cup) freezer-proof container. Cover and freeze for 6–8 hours, or until set.

Use a metal spoon to break up the frozen mixture. Quickly transfer to the bowl of a food processor and process to a soft, icy texture (don't over-process or the sorbet will begin to melt). Immediately return the sorbet to the container, cover and refreeze for 4–6 hours, or until completely frozen.

Serve small scoops of the sorbet with the cream passed separately to dollop on top.

This sorbet will keep, stored in an airtight container in the freezer, for up to 2 weeks.

Turkish delight and pistachio rocky road bites

Line the base and long sides of a 16 x 26 cm (6¼ x 10½ inch) baking tin with baking paper, allowing the paper to overhang the sides.

Place the chocolate in a heatproof bowl over a saucepan of simmering water, ensuring the bowl doesn't touch the water. Stir until the chocolate has melted. Remove from the heat and set aside, stirring occasionally, to cool to room temperature.

Add the Turkish delight, coconut and pistachio nuts to the cooled chocolate and stir to combine. Spoon into the prepared tin and use the back of the spoon to spread evenly. Lightly tap the tin on the bench to settle the mixture. Stand in a cool place for 1–4 hours, or until the chocolate has set (this will depend on the weather).

Transfer the rocky road to a cutting board. Use a 3 cm (1¼ inch) cookie cutter dipped in cornflour to cut into rounds. Dust with the sugar, if desired, and place in small paper cases to serve.

These rocky road bites will keep, stored in an airtight container in a cool place, for up to 1 month.

MAKES ABOUT 36

400 g (14 oz) dark chocolate (54 per cent cocoa solids), chopped
110 g (3¾ oz) Turkish delight, cubed
60 g (2¼ oz/1 cup) shredded coconut
100 g (3½ oz/¾ cup) pistachio nuts, lightly toasted and coarsely chopped
icing (confectioners') sugar, sifted, for dusting (optional)

Flourless bitter chocolate hearts

MAKES 6

50 g (1¾ oz) dark chocolate (70 per cent cocoa solids), chopped
60 g (2¼ oz/¼ cup) unsalted butter
2 eggs, at room temperature, separated
55 g (2 oz/¼ cup) caster (superfine) sugar
1 tablespoon brandy
55 g (2 oz/½ cup) ground almonds
thick (double/heavy) cream
300 g (10½ oz) mixed fresh or thawed frozen berries

Chocolate glaze
150 g (5½ oz) dark chocolate (70 per cent cocoa solids powder), chopped
60 g (2¼ oz/¼ cup) unsalted butter, chopped

Preheat the oven to 160°C (315°F/Gas 2–3). Grease a six-hole heart-shaped tin or a giant muffin tin. Line the bases with baking paper, cut to fit.

Combine the chocolate and butter in a heatproof bowl over a saucepan of simmering water, ensuring the bowl doesn't touch the water. Stir until the chocolate and butter have melted. Remove from the heat.

Lightly whisk the egg yolks with a fork. Add to the chocolate mixture with the sugar, brandy and ground almonds. Stir with a wooden spoon to combine.

Beat the egg whites in a separate bowl using electric beaters until stiff peaks form. To loosen the mixture, using a large metal spoon or spatula, fold a spoonful of the egg whites into the chocolate mixture. Fold in the remaining egg whites. Spoon into the prepared tin and bake for 20 minutes, or until a skewer inserted in the centre of a cake comes out clean. Set aside to cool completely in the tin.

To make the chocolate glaze, combine the chocolate and butter in a heatproof bowl over a saucepan of simmering water, ensuring the bowl doesn't touch the water. Stir until the chocolate and butter have melted. Transfer to a jug.

Place a wire rack over a baking tray. Turn the cakes out onto the wire rack, base side up. Slowly pour the chocolate glaze over the cakes, allowing it to drizzle down the sides. Use a spatula to spread, if necessary. Gently tap the rack on the bench to settle the glaze. Stand the cakes in a cool place until the glaze has set. Serve accompanied by the cream and berries.

The unglazed cakes will keep, stored in a single layer in an airtight container in a cool place, for up to 3 days. Once glazed, they will keep, stored in an airtight container at room temperature, for up to 1 day.

Hazelnut meringues with chocolate ganache

MAKES 12

100 g (3½ oz) hazelnuts, toasted and skinned
4 egg whites, at room temperature
pinch of salt
230 g (8 oz/1 cup) caster (superfine) sugar
60 g (2¼ oz) dark chocolate (54 per cent cocoa solids), chopped
10 g (¼ oz) unsalted butter, cubed
cream (optional)

Chocolate ganache
150 g (5½ oz) dark chocolate (54 per cent cocoa solids), chopped
125 ml (4 fl oz/½ cup) cream
1½ tablespoons Frangelico

Preheat the oven to 100°C (200°F/Gas ½). Draw two 12 x 20 cm (4½ x 8 inch) rectangles each on three pieces of baking paper and place on three baking trays, with the pencil marks facing down.

Place the hazelnuts in the bowl of a food processor and process until finely ground.

Beat the egg whites and salt in a large bowl using electric beaters until soft peaks form. Add the sugar, a spoonful at a time, and beat until very thick and glossy and all the sugar has dissolved. Use a large metal spoon or spatula to fold the ground hazelnuts into the meringue mixture. Divide the meringue evenly among the marked rectangles on the prepared trays and use the back of a spoon to spread out evenly. Bake, rotating the trays every 20 minutes, for 1 hour, or until crisp. Turn off the oven and leave the meringue rectangles in the oven for 2 hours, or until cooled to room temperature.

Meanwhile, to make the chocolate ganache, combine the chocolate and cream in a small saucepan over low heat and stir until the chocolate has melted. Stir in the Frangelico, and then set aside to cool to a thin, spreadable consistency.

Spread half the chocolate ganache over two of the meringue rectangles. Top each with another meringue rectangle, spread on the remaining ganache and finish with a layer of meringue, to form two meringue stacks. Cover with plastic wrap and place in the refrigerator for 30 minutes, or until the ganache is firm.

Place the chocolate and butter in a heatproof bowl over a saucepan of simmering water, ensuring the bowl doesn't touch the water. Stir until the chocolate has melted.

Carefully transfer the meringue stacks to a cutting board. Use a sharp knife to cut each stack into six slices. Drizzle with the chocolate and butter mixture and stand at room temperature for at least 30 minutes.

Serve accompanied by the cream, if desired.

These hazelnut meringues with chocolate ganache will keep, stored in an airtight container at room temperature, for up to 2 days.

White chocolate and lime truffles

Place the cream and half the chocolate in a heatproof bowl over a saucepan of simmering water, ensuring the bowl doesn't touch the water. Stir until the chocolate has melted. Remove from the heat, add the grated zest, cover and chill for 30 minutes.

Grease a 17 cm (6½ inch) square cake tin and line the base and sides with baking paper. Line a tray with baking paper.

Beat the chocolate mixture using electric beaters for 3 minutes. Spoon into the prepared tin and smooth the surface with the back of a spoon. Chill for 2 hours, or until firm.

Turn out the chocolate mixture onto a cutting board. Trim the edges, then cut into 2.5 cm (1 inch) squares. Transfer the squares to the prepared tray. Freeze for 20 minutes.

Meanwhile, place the remaining chocolate in a heatproof bowl over a saucepan of simmering water, ensuring the bowl doesn't touch the water. Stir until the chocolate has melted. Remove from the heat.

Using two forks, dip the chocolate squares, one at a time, into the melted chocolate, allowing any excess to drip off. Return to the tray, immediately place a strip of lime zest on each square and stand in a cool place until the chocolate has set.

These truffles will keep, stored in a single layer in an airtight container in a cool place, for up to 2 days.

MAKES 36

80 ml (2½ fl oz/⅓ cup) thickened
   (whipping) cream
600 g (1 lb 5 oz) white chocolate, chopped
3 teaspoons finely grated lime zest
lime zest strips, to decorate

Striped chocolate fingers

MAKES ABOUT 70

100 g (3½ oz) unsalted butter, softened
75 g (2¾ oz/⅓ cup) sugar
1 teaspoon natural vanilla extract
1 egg, at room temperature
125 g (4½ oz/1 cup) plain (all-purpose) flour
½ teaspoon baking powder
1 tablespoon unsweetened cocoa powder, sifted
1 tablespoon plain (all-purpose) flour, extra, sifted

Cream the butter, sugar and vanilla in a medium-sized bowl using electric beaters until pale and fluffy. Add the egg and beat until just combined. Sift in the flour and baking powder and stir until a soft dough forms.

Divide the dough in half and transfer to a lightly floured work surface. Gently knead the cocoa into one portion and the extra flour into the other portion. Divide each portion of dough in half, cover with plastic wrap and refrigerate until firm.

Line a baking tray with baking paper. Roll out each portion of dough on a lightly floured work surface to form a 7.5 x 25 cm (3 x 10 inch) rectangle. Place a chocolate rectangle on the prepared tray, top with a plain rectangle and press down lightly. Repeat with the remaining rectangle layers, finishing with a plain layer. Cover with plastic wrap and chill for 2 hours.

Preheat the oven to 160°C (315°F/Gas 2–3). Line two baking trays with baking paper.

Transfer the dough block to a cutting board. Trim the edges, then cut into 3 mm (1/8 inch) thick slices. Place the slices about 1.5 cm (5/8 inch) apart on the prepared trays. Bake, swapping the trays halfway through cooking, for 15 minutes, or until the biscuits just start to colour. Allow to cool on the trays.

These fingers will keep, stored in an airtight container, for up to 2 weeks.

White chocolate and pomegranate brûlée

Place six 125 ml (4 fl oz/½ cup) ramekins on a tray.

Combine the milk and cream in a saucepan over medium heat and bring almost to a simmer. Remove from the heat.

Meanwhile, whisk the egg yolks in a medium-sized bowl until just combined. Gradually whisk in the hot milk mixture. Return to the clean saucepan and cook over low heat, whisking constantly, for 5 minutes, or until the custard thickens enough to coat the back of a wooden spoon. Remove from the heat, add the chocolate and stir until the chocolate has melted. Strain into a jug.

Divide the pomegranate pulp among the ramekins and pour on the custard. Place in the refrigerator for 6–8 hours, or until lightly set and a skin has formed on the surface.

At least 1 hour before serving, make the toffee. Combine the sugar and water in a small heavy-based saucepan over low heat and stir until the sugar has dissolved. Bring to the boil and simmer, without stirring, until the syrup turns golden brown. Remove from the heat and allow the bubbles to subside, then carefully pour over the custards. Return to the refrigerator and chill before serving.

These brûlées, without the toffee topping, will keep, covered with plastic wrap or stored in an airtight container in the refrigerator, for up to 2 days.

MAKES 6

310 ml (10¾ fl oz/1¼ cups) milk
300 ml (10½ fl oz) thickened cream
6 egg yolks
250 g (9 oz) white chocolate, finely chopped
150 g (5½ oz/⅔ cup) pomegranate pulp

Toffee
110 g (3¾ oz/½ cup) sugar
2 tablespoons water

Cherry and almond chocolate bark

MAKES 25

200 g (7 oz) dark chocolate (70 per cent cocoa solids), chopped
55 g (2 oz/⅓ cup) dried cherries
40 g (1½ oz/¼ cup) slivered almonds, lightly toasted

Line a tray with baking paper.

Place the chocolate in a heatproof bowl over a saucepan of simmering water, ensuring the bowl doesn't touch the water. Stir until the chocolate has melted. Remove from the heat.

Pour the chocolate onto the prepared tray and spread evenly into a 20 cm (8 inch) square. Tap the tray on the bench to settle the chocolate. Sprinkle on the cherries and almonds. Stand in a cool place for 3–4 hours, or until the chocolate has set.

Break the chocolate bark into rough 4 cm (1½ inch) pieces.

This chocolate bark will keep, stored in an airtight container in a cool spot, for up to 2 weeks.

TIPS: Dried cherries are available from selected health food and gourmet food stores. You can replace the dried cherries with sweetened dried cranberries, if you wish.
Toast the almonds in a preheated 180°C (350°F/Gas 4) oven for 5 minutes, or until lightly golden and aromatic. Allow to cool on the tray.

Pears poached in spiced chocolate syrup

Combine the sugar and cocoa in a saucepan. Gradually stir in the water, add the golden syrup, star anise, cinnamon and peppercorns and stir over medium heat until the sugar has dissolved. Bring to a simmer.

Meanwhile, starting at the base of each the pear, remove the cores with an apple corer, leaving the stems intact. If necessary, trim the base of the pears slightly so they stand upright. Peel the pears and add to the syrup and simmer gently, uncovered and turning the pears occasionally, for 10–15 minutes, or until the pears are just tender when tested with a skewer. Use a slotted spoon to transfer the pears to a plate or dish. Cover with foil to keep warm and set aside.

Bring the syrup to the boil and simmer, without stirring, for 30 minutes, or until thick, syrupy and reduced by three-quarters.

Serve the pears accompanied by the syrup and ice cream or cream.

SERVES 4

165 g (5¾ oz/¾ cup) sugar
40 g (1½ oz/⅓ cup) unsweetened cocoa powder, sifted
1.5 litres (52 fl oz/6 cups) water
3 tablespoons golden syrup (light treacle)
2 star anise
2 cinnamon sticks
1 teaspoon black peppercorns
4 firm ripe pears, such as beurre bosc
vanilla ice cream or lightly whipped cream

White chocolate and macadamia biscotti

MAKES ABOUT 70

180 g (6¼ oz) unsalted butter, melted
and cooled
230 g (8¼ oz/1 cup) caster (superfine) sugar
3 eggs, at room temperature
finely grated zest of 3 lemons
1 teaspoon natural vanilla extract
200 g (7 oz) white chocolate, chopped
120 g (4¼ oz) macadamia nut halves
375 g (13 oz/3 cups) plain (all-purpose) flour
1 teaspoon baking powder

Preheat the oven to 160°C (315°F/Gas 2–3). Line two baking trays with baking paper.

Combine the melted butter, sugar, eggs, lemon zest and vanilla in a large bowl and whisk with a fork until well combined. Stir in the chocolate and macadamia nuts. In a separate bowl, sift together the flour and baking powder. Add to the butter mixture and stir with a wooden spoon to form a soft, slightly sticky dough. Divide the mixture into four equal portions. Transfer each portion to a lightly floured work surface and shape into a 5 x 20 cm (2 x 8 inch) log. Place on the prepared trays 7 cm (2¾ inches) apart, allowing room for spreading, and flatten each log slightly with your hands. Bake, swapping the trays halfway through cooking, for 30–35 minutes, or until the logs are firm to touch and are just cooked through. Set aside to cool on the trays.

Reduce the oven temperature to 150°C (300°F/Gas 2). Use a sharp knife to cut two logs diagonally into 1 cm (½ inch) thick slices. Spread the biscotti well apart on the trays. Bake, turning them over halfway through cooking, for 20 minutes, or until the biscotti are crisp and just starting to colour. Allow to cool on the trays. Repeat with the remaining logs.

These biscotti will keep, stored in an airtight container, for up to 2 weeks.

Chocolate petits pots de crème

Preheat the oven to 170°C (325°F/Gas 3).

Combine the cream and milk in a small saucepan over low heat and bring almost to a simmer. Remove from the heat, add the chocolate and stir until melted.

Whisk the egg yolks, sugar and vanilla in a medium-sized bowl until just combined. Stir in the chocolate mixture and strain into a jug.

Divide the mixture among six 125 ml (4 fl oz/½ cup) ramekins. Place the ramekins in an ovenproof dish and add enough boiling water to come halfway up the side of the ramekins. Bake for 25–30 minutes, or until the centres wobble slightly when the ramekins are lightly tapped.

Remove the ramekins from the water bath and cool at room temperature for 1 hour. Cover each ramekin with plastic wrap and place in the refrigerator for 2–3 hours, or until chilled. Serve dusted with the cocoa.

These custards will keep, covered in the refrigerator, for up to 2 days.

TIP: Use dark chocolate (70 per cent cocoa solids) for a more intensely chocolate-flavoured custard.

SERVES 6

250 ml (9 fl oz/1 cup) cream
125 ml (4 fl oz/½ cup) milk
100 g (3½ oz) dark chocolate (54 per cent cocoa solids), chopped
5 egg yolks, at room temperature
55 g (2 oz/¼ cup) caster (superfine) sugar
1 teaspoon natural vanilla extract
unsweetened cocoa powder, sifted, for dusting

The high life

Chocolate
chestnut roulade

MAKES 10

150 g (5½ oz) dark chocolate (54 per cent
cocoa solids)
60 ml (2 fl oz/¼ cup) water
4 eggs, at room temperature, separated
80 g (2¾ oz/⅓ cup) caster (superfine) sugar
2 tablespoons plain (all-purpose) flour, sifted
1 tablespoon unsweetened cocoa powder, sifted,
for dusting

Chestnut filling
170 g (6 oz/½ cup) sweetened chestnut purée
125 ml (4 fl oz/½ cup) thickened
(whipping) cream, lightly whipped

Chocolate sauce
125 g (4½ oz) dark chocolate (54 per cent cocoa
solids), chopped
160 ml (5¼ fl oz) cream

Preheat the oven to 180°C (350°F/Gas 4). Grease a 25 x 38 cm (10 x 15 inch) baking tray and line with baking paper, cutting into the corners to fit, allowing the paper to extend at least 2 cm (¾ inch) beyond the edges of the tray.

Combine the chocolate and water in a small saucepan over low heat and stir until the chocolate has melted. Remove from the heat.

Beat the egg yolks and sugar in a large bowl using electric beaters until pale and thick. Fold in the chocolate mixture using a large metal spoon or spatula, then fold in the flour.

In a separate bowl, beat the egg whites using electric beaters until soft peaks form. To loosen the mixture, fold a large spoonful of the egg whites into the chocolate mixture. Fold in the remaining egg whites. Pour onto the prepared tray and smooth the surface. Tap the tray gently on the bench to settle the mixture.

Bake for 10 minutes, or until a skewer inserted into the centre comes out clean. Place the tray on a wire rack and cover the cake with a piece of baking paper and a clean damp tea towel (dish towel). Set aside for 30 minutes.

Meanwhile, to make the chestnut filling, beat the chestnut purée in a medium-sized bowl using electric beaters until soft. Fold in the cream until swirled through.

Cut a piece of baking paper slightly larger than the cake. Place on a cutting board and dust evenly with the cocoa. Remove the tea towel and paper from the cake. Turn the cake out onto the cocoa-dusted baking paper, so that a long side is facing you, and remove the lining paper. Use a sharp knife to cut the cake, and the baking paper underneath, in half to form two 19 x 25 cm (7½ x 10 inch) rectangles. Spread the chestnut filling evenly over the cakes. Starting at the end closest to you and using the baking paper as a guide, firmly roll one of the cake halves up to form a roulade.

Wrap the baking paper firmly around the roulade and place, seam side down, on a tray. Repeat with the remaining cake half. Transfer to the refrigerator for 2 hours, or until firm.

To make the chocolate sauce, combine the chocolate and cream in a small saucepan over low heat and stir until the chocolate has melted. Remove from the heat and set aside.

To serve, reheat the chocolate sauce over low heat, if necessary. Remove the baking paper from the roulades, dust with cocoa (see pic) and cut each into five slices. Serve drizzled with the warm chocolate sauce.

This roulade will keep, covered with plastic wrap in the refrigerator, for up to 2 days. The chocolate sauce will keep, stored in an airtight container in the refrigerator, for up to 5 days.

Chocolate caramel tartlets

MAKES 42

200 g (7 oz) dark chocolate, chopped
30 g (1 oz) unsalted butter, cubed

Tart case
110 g (3¾ oz) plain (all-purpose) flour
½ teaspoon baking powder
90 g (3¼ oz/1 cup) desiccated coconut
95 g (3¼ oz/½ cup) soft brown sugar
125 g (4½ oz/½ cup) unsalted butter, melted
1 teaspoon natural vanilla extract

Caramel filling
395 g (14 oz) tin sweetened condensed milk
95 g (3½ oz/½ cup) soft brown sugar
80 g (2¾ oz) unsalted butter, cubed
2 tablespoons golden syrup (light treacle)

Preheat the oven to 180°C (350°F/Gas 4). Grease 42 holes of four 12-hole mini muffin tins.

To make the tart cases, sift the flour and baking powder into a medium-sized bowl, add the coconut and sugar and stir with a wooden spoon. Stir in the butter and vanilla until combined. Divide the mixture evenly among the prepared tins, pressing firmly into the bases and sides. Bake for 12 minutes, or until light golden and crisp.

To make the caramel filling, combine the condensed milk, sugar, butter and golden syrup in a heavy-based saucepan over low heat and stir until the sugar has dissolved. Bring to a simmer and cook, stirring constantly, for 5 minutes, or until the mixture darkens slightly.

Immediately spoon the caramel filling into the tartlet cases. Bake for 5–8 minutes, or until the caramel is bubbling around the edges. Allow to cool in the tins for 10 minutes, then use a small spatula to transfer the tartlets to a wire rack to cool completely.

To make the chocolate topping, combine the chocolate and butter in a heatproof bowl over a saucepan of simmering water, ensuring the bowl doesn't touch the water. Stir until the chocolate and butter have melted. Remove from the heat. Spread a thick layer of chocolate evenly over the top of the tartlets. Stand in a cool place for 4–6 hours, or until the chocolate has set.

These tartlets will keep, stored in an airtight container, for up to 2 weeks.

After-eights

These recipes are truly, madly, deeply decadent.

Chocolate, date and walnut tortes

MAKES 8

vegetable oil, to grease
4 egg whites, at room temperature
80 g (2¾ oz/⅓ cup) caster (superfine) sugar
150 g (5½ oz) dark chocolate (54 per cent cocoa solids), chopped
150 g (5½ oz/1½ cups) walnut halves, chopped
120 g (4¼ oz/⅔ cup) pitted dates, chopped
1 tablespoon unsweetened cocoa powder, sifted
whipping cream, lightly whipped, to serve

Preheat the oven to 160°C (315°F/Gas 2–3). Brush eight 8 cm (3¼ inch) loose-based fluted flan (tart) tins with the oil and line the bases with rounds of baking paper. Place the tins on a baking tray.

Beat the egg whites in a large bowl using electric beaters until soft peaks form. Add the sugar, a tablespoon at a time, and beat until thick and glossy.

Use a large metal spoon or spatula to fold the chocolate, walnuts, dates and cocoa into the meringue mixture. Divide the mixture among the prepared tins and smooth the surfaces with the back of a spoon. Bake for 40 minutes, or until the tortes start to pull away slightly from the edge of the tins. Turn off the oven and allow the tortes to cool in the oven with the door slightly ajar.

Remove the tortes from the tins and transfer to serving plates. Serve accompanied by the cream.

These tortes will keep, stored in an airtight container, for up to 2 days.

Triple chocolate fudge cookies

Place the dark chocolate in a heatproof bowl over a saucepan of simmering water, ensuring the bowl doesn't touch the water. Stir until the chocolate has melted. Set aside, stirring occasionally, until cooled to room temperature.

Cream the butter and sugar in a large bowl using electric beaters until pale and fluffy. Add the eggs one at a time, beating well after each addition. Beat in the cooled, melted chocolate. Sift in the flours, add the milk chocolate and white chocolate and, using a wooden spoon, stir to combine. Cover with plastic wrap and refrigerate for 1 hour, or until firm enough to roll.

Preheat the oven to 180°C (350°F/Gas 4). Line a baking tray with baking paper.

Roll tablespoons of the mixture into balls, place on the prepared tray 5 cm (2 inches) apart and flatten slightly. Bake for 10 minutes, or until the cookies are still slightly soft to touch. Allow to cool on the tray for 5 minutes, then transfer to a wire rack to cool completely. Repeat with the remaining mixture.

These cookies will keep, stored in an airtight container, for up to 1 week.

MAKES ABOUT 35

200 g (7 oz) dark chocolate, chopped
125 g (4½ oz) unsalted butter, softened
115 g (4 oz/½ cup) soft brown sugar
2 eggs, at room temperature
155 g (5½ oz/1¼ cups) plain (all-purpose) flour
40 g (1½ oz/⅓ cup) self-raising flour
125 g (4½ oz) good-quality milk chocolate, roughly chopped
125 g (4½ oz) good-quality white chocolate, roughly chopped

Molten chocolate puddings with malt cream

MAKES 6

200 g (7 oz) dark chocolate (54 per cent cocoa
solids), chopped
100 g (3½ oz) unsalted butter, cubed
2 eggs, at room temperature
2 egg yolks, at room temperature
55 g (2 oz/¼ cup) caster (superfine) sugar
2 tablespoons plain (all-purpose) flour, sifted
unsweetened cocoa powder, sifted, for dusting

Malt cream

200 ml (7 fl oz) whipping cream
45 g (1¾ oz/⅓ cup) malted milk powder
1 tablespoon icing (confectioners') sugar, sifted

Preheat the oven to 180°C (350°F/Gas 4). Grease six
185 ml (6 fl oz/¾ cup) pudding basins (moulds).
Place on a baking tray.

Combine the chocolate and butter in a small saucepan
over low heat and stir until melted. Remove from
the heat.

Beat the eggs, egg yolks and caster sugar in a
medium-sized bowl using electric beaters until pale
and creamy. Use a large metal spoon or spatula to fold
in the chocolate mixture and the flour. Spoon into the
prepared basins and bake for 12 minutes, or until the
puddings have risen almost to the top of the basins
(they will still look slightly underdone).

Meanwhile, to make the malt cream, place the cream,
milk powder and sugar in a medium-sized bowl and
whisk until soft peaks form. Cover with plastic wrap
and place in the refrigerator until required.

Run a flat-bladed knife around the edge of the
puddings and turn out onto serving plates. Serve
immediately, dusted with the cocoa and accompanied
by the malt cream.

Chocolate and Frangelico frappé

Combine the ice, milk, cream, Frangelico, sugar and cocoa in a blender and blend until thick and creamy. Pour into two tall glasses and serve immediately dusted with the extra cocoa.

TIP: You can omit the Frangelico if you wish or even replace it with another liqueur, such as Tia Maria or Kahlua.

SERVES 2

270 g (9½ oz/2 cups) ice cubes
125 ml (4 fl oz/½ cup) milk
60 ml (2 fl oz/¼ cup) cream
2 tablespoons Frangelico
30 g (1 oz/¼ cup) icing (confectioners') sugar
2 tablespoons unsweetened cocoa powder, plus extra, sifted, for dusting

Chocolate martini

SERVES 2

crushed ice
80 ml (2½ fl oz/⅓ cup) chocolate liqueur
60 ml (2 fl oz/¼ cup) vodka
2 chocolate sticks, to garnish

Half fill a cocktail shaker with the ice. Add the chocolate liqueur and vodka and shake vigorously until well combined. Strain into two chilled martini glasses, garnish each with a chocolate stick and serve immediately.

Mini chocolate fruit cakes

MAKES 12

80 ml (2½ fl oz/⅓ cup) sweet Marsala
or Tia Maria
2 tablespoons water
2 teaspoons instant coffee granules
150 g (5½ oz) pitted prunes, chopped
150 g (5½ oz) pitted dates, chopped
100 g (3½ oz)' dried dessert figs, chopped
100 g (3½ oz) sultanas (golden raisins)
125 g (4½ oz/½ cup) unsalted butter, softened
115 g (4 oz/½ cup) soft brown sugar
2 eggs, at room temperature
90 g (3¼ oz/¾ cup) plain (all-purpose) flour
2 tablespoons unsweetened cocoa powder
½ teaspoon baking powder
150 g (5½ oz) dark chocolate (54 per cent
cocoa solids), chopped
1½ tablespoons sweet Marsala
or Tia Maria, extra
icing (confectioners') sugar, sifted, for dusting

Combine the Marsala or Tia Maria and water in a small saucepan over medium heat and bring to just below simmering point. Remove from the heat and add the coffee, stirring to dissolve. Add the prunes, dates, figs and sultanas and stir to combine. Set aside, stirring occasionally, for 1 hour, or until the liquid has been absorbed.

Preheat the oven to 160°C (315°F/Gas 2–3). Grease a 12-hole friand tin.

Cream the butter and brown sugar in a large bowl using electric beaters until pale and fluffy. Add the eggs, one at a time, beating well after each addition. Sift the flour, cocoa and baking powder into a separate bowl. Fold half of the flour mixture into the butter mixture. Add the fruit mixture and the chocolate and stir until just combined. Fold in the remaining flour mixture. Divide the mixture among the friand moulds and smooth the surfaces with the back of a spoon. Bake for 45 minutes, or until cooked when tested with a skewer. Drizzle the still-hot cakes with the extra Marsala or Tia Maria, then set aside to cool. Serve dusted with the icing sugar.

These cakes will keep, stored in an airtight container, for up to 2 weeks.

TIP: These dense, rich cakes make a great gift.

Chocolate cherry trifles

SERVES 6

170 g (6 oz/¾ cup) caster (superfine) sugar
2 tablespoons unsweetened cocoa powder, sifted
170 ml (5½ fl oz/⅔ cup) water
2 tablespoons brandy or kirsch
300 g (10½ oz) pitted fresh or thawed frozen
  cherries, halved
300 ml (10½ fl oz) whipping cream
2 tablespoons icing (confectioners') sugar
110 g (3¾ oz/½ cup) mascarpone cheese
15 savoiardi (lady fingers), broken into chunks
160 g (5¾ oz/½ cup) cherry jam
45 g (1¾ oz/½ cup) flaked almonds,
  lightly toasted

Combine the caster sugar and cocoa in a small saucepan and gradually stir in the water and brandy or kirsch. Place over medium heat and stir until the sugar dissolves. Add the cherries and bring to a simmer, stirring occasionally. Simmer for 1–2 minutes, then remove from the heat. Strain, reserving the chocolate syrup, and set aside.

Whip the cream and icing sugar in a bowl using electric beaters until soft peaks form. Whisk in the mascarpone until just combined.

Divide half the savoiardi among six 310 ml (10¾ fl oz/1¼ cup) glasses or serving dishes and drizzle with half the reserved chocolate syrup. Top with half the poached cherries, half the cream and then half the jam and half the almonds. Repeat the layers with the remaining savoiardi, chocolate syrup, cherries, cream and jam, reserving the remaining almonds. Cover with plastic wrap and place in the refrigerator for at least 2 hours. Serve sprinkled with the reserved almonds.

These trifles will keep, stored in the refrigerator, for up to 2 days.

TIPS: Savoiardi are also known as sponge finger biscuits (cookies) and are available from the sweet biscuit section of the supermarket. Toast the almonds in a preheated 180°C (350°F/Gas 4) oven for 6 minutes, or until lightly golden and aromatic. Allow to cool on the tray.

White chocolate and raspberry cheesecakes

SERVES 8

125 g (4½ oz) plain sweet biscuits (cookies)
90 g (3¼ oz/⅓ cup) unsalted butter, melted
150 g (5½ oz) raspberries, to serve

Filling

125 g (4½ oz) white chocolate, chopped
125 ml (4 fl oz/½ cup) cream
200 g (7 oz) cream cheese
185 g (6½ oz/¾ cup) sour cream
55 g (2 oz/¼ cup) caster (superfine) sugar
3 eggs, at room temperature
300 g (10½ oz) frozen raspberries, thawed

Preheat the oven to 150°C (300°F/Gas 2). Line eight holes of two six-hole giant muffin tins with paper cases.

Place the biscuits in the bowl of a food processor and process until finely crushed. Add the melted butter and process until combined. Spoon into the prepared tins and press down firmly with the back of a spoon. Chill until required.

To make the filling, place the chocolate and cream in a small saucepan over low heat and stir until the chocolate has melted. Remove from the heat and allow to cool. Place the cream cheese in the cleaned bowl of the food processor and process until smooth. Add the sour cream, sugar, eggs and chocolate mixture and process until smooth. Gently stir in the raspberries.

Spoon the filling into the tins. Bake for 40 minutes, or until just set and the centres wobble slightly. Turn off the oven and leave the door slightly ajar, allowing the cheesecakes to cool for 1 hour. Remove from the oven and allow to cool completely in the tins on a wire rack.

Chill for 2 hours before serving. Remove the cheesecakes from the tins and serve with the raspberries.

These cheesecakes will keep, stored in an airtight container in the refrigerator, for up to 3 days.

Chocolate pecan and golden syrup tarts

MAKES 6

unsweetened cocoa powder or icing
(confectioners') sugar, sifted, for dusting

Chocolate pastry
185 g (6½ oz/1½ cups) plain (all-purpose)
flour, sifted
2 tablespoons unsweetened cocoa powder, sifted
2 tablespoons icing (confectioners') sugar, sifted
150 g (5½ oz) unsalted butter, chilled and cubed
2 tablespoons chilled water

Filling
75 g (2¾ oz) dark chocolate (54 per cent cocoa
solids), chopped
75 g (2¾ oz) unsalted butter, cubed
1 egg, at room temperature
1 egg yolk, at room temperature
2 tablespoons golden syrup (light treacle)
1½ tablespoons caster (superfine) sugar
50 g (1¾ oz/½ cup) pecans, lightly toasted
and chopped

To make the chocolate pastry, combine the flour, cocoa, sugar and butter in the bowl of a food processor and process until the mixture resembles fine breadcrumbs. Add the water and pulse until just combined. Turn out onto a lightly floured work surface and knead for 1–2 minutes, or until the dough just comes together. Divide the dough in half and shape each portion into a disc. Cover with plastic wrap and refrigerate for 15 minutes.

Roll out one portion of dough to 3 mm (⅛ inch) thick. Cut out three 12 cm (4½ inch) rounds, re-rolling if necessary. Line three 8 cm (3¼ inch) loose-based fluted flan (tart) tins and trim the edges. Repeat with the remaining dough. Transfer the tins to a baking tray and freeze for 40 minutes.

Preheat the oven to 200°C (400°F/Gas 6). Bake the pastry cases for 15 minutes, or until just cooked and dry.

Meanwhile, to make the filling, place the chocolate and butter in a small saucepan over low heat and stir until melted. Remove from the heat. Combine the egg,

egg yolk, golden syrup and sugar in a medium-sized bowl and whisk well. Stir in the chocolate mixture and transfer to a jug.

Reduce the oven temperature to 180°C (350°F/Gas 4). Pour the chocolate mixture into the warm pastry cases, then sprinkle on the pecans. Bake for 15 minutes, or until the filling is puffed.

Serve warm, dusted with the cocoa or sugar.

These tarts will keep, stored in an airtight container, for up to 4 days.

Frozen chocolate puddings with Brazil nut toffee

MAKES 6

canola or vegetable oil, to grease
60 g (2¼ oz) white chocolate, chopped
185 ml (6 fl oz/¾ cup) milk
1 teaspoon natural vanilla extract
60 g (2¼ oz) milk chocolate, chopped
50 g (1¾ oz) dark chocolate (70 per cent cocoa solids), chopped
3 egg yolks
115 g (4 oz/½ cup) caster (superfine) sugar
250 ml (9 fl oz/1 cup) whipping cream

Brazil nut toffee
50 g (1¾ oz/⅓ cup) Brazil nuts, lightly toasted, skinned and sliced
170 g (6 oz/½ cup) caster (superfine) sugar
2 tablespoons water

Brush six 125 ml (4 fl oz/½ cup) dariole moulds with the oil. Place the moulds on a tray.

Combine the white chocolate and 60 ml (2 fl oz/¼ cup) of the milk in a heatproof bowl over a saucepan of simmering water, ensuring the bowl doesn't touch the water. Stir until the chocolate has melted. Remove from the heat, stir in the vanilla and set aside. Repeat this procedure with the milk chocolate and 60 ml (2 fl oz/¼ cup) of the milk, and the dark chocolate and the remaining milk, each in separate heatproof bowls.

Place the egg yolks and sugar in a heatproof bowl over a saucepan of simmering water, ensuring the bowl doesn't touch the water. Beat using electric beaters until pale and very thick. Remove from the heat and beat until cooled to room temperature. Divide the mixture evenly among the three chocolate mixtures and stir until combined.

Whip the cream in a medium-sized bowl using electric beaters until soft peaks form. Divide the cream among each bowl of chocolate and fold in to combine.

Spoon the dark chocolate mixture into the prepared moulds and smooth the surfaces with the back of a spoon. Transfer to the refrigerator for 30 minutes. Carefully top with the milk chocolate mixture, chill for 30 minutes, then finish with a layer of the white chocolate mixture. Place in the freezer for 4–6 hours, or until set.

Meanwhile, to make the Brazil nut toffee, line a baking tray with baking paper. Spread the Brazil nuts on the prepared tray close together. Combine the sugar and water in a small heavy-based saucepan and stir over low heat until the sugar has dissolved. Increase the heat to medium and simmer, without stirring, until the syrup is golden. Remove immediately from the heat and allow the bubbles to subside. Pour over the Brazil nuts and set aside to cool. Break the toffee into shards.

Dip the moulds, one at a time, into a bowl of hot water for 5 seconds. Slide a palette knife down the side of each mould to create an air pocket, then turn out onto serving plates. Serve with the Brazil nut toffee. These puddings will keep in the moulds, covered with foil, in the freezer for up to 2 weeks. The toffee will keep in an airtight container at room temperature for up to 5 days.

TIP: Toast the Brazil nuts in a preheated 180°C (350°F/Gas 4) for 10 minutes, or until lightly golden and aromatic. Allow to cool on the tray.

Double chocolate mud brownies

MAKES 25

250 g (9 oz) dark chocolate (54 per cent cocoa
   solids), chopped
150 g (5½ oz) unsalted butter, cubed
170 g (6 oz/¾ cup) caster (superfine) sugar
3 eggs, at room temperature, lightly whisked
60 g (2¼ oz/½ cup) plain (all-purpose) flour
½ teaspoon baking powder
150 g (5½ oz) milk chocolate, roughly chopped
unsweetened cocoa powder or icing
   (confectioners') sugar, sifted, for dusting

Preheat the oven to 160°C (315°F/Gas 2–3). Grease a 20 cm (8 inch) square cake tin and line the base and two opposite sides with baking paper, extending the paper over the sides for easy removal later.

Place the dark chocolate and butter in a heatproof bowl over a saucepan of simmering water, ensuring the bowl doesn't touch the water. Stir until the chocolate and butter have melted. Remove from the heat and set aside to cool to lukewarm.

Add the sugar and eggs to the chocolate mixture and whisk until well combined. Sift in the flour and baking powder and whisk until just combined, then, using a wooden spoon, stir in the milk chocolate. Pour into the prepared tin and bake for 45–50 minutes, or until moist crumbs cling to a skewer inserted in the centre. Set aside to cool in the tin.

Remove the brownie from the tin, using the baking paper. Cut into 4 cm (1½ inch) squares. Dust with the cocoa or icing sugar and serve.

These brownies will keep, stored in an airtight container at room temperature, for up to 5 days.

Chocolate
French toast

SERVES 2

60 g (2¼ oz) dark chocolate (54 per cent cocoa solids)
4 x 1.5 cm (⅝ inch) thick slices day-old brioche
1 egg, at room temperature
1½ tablespoons cream
1½ tablespoons milk
1 tablespoon caster (superfine) sugar
½ teaspoon natural vanilla extract
¼ teaspoon ground cinnamon
20 g (¾ oz) butter
icing (confectioners') sugar, sifted, for dusting

Place the chocolate in a heatproof bowl over a saucepan of simmering water, ensuring the bowl doesn't touch the water. Stir until the chocolate has melted. Remove from the heat.

Spread two slices of brioche with the melted chocolate and sandwich together with the remaining slices.

Whisk the egg, cream, milk, caster sugar, vanilla and cinnamon with a fork in a shallow bowl.

Soak the sandwiches in the egg mixture for 30 seconds on each side. Meanwhile, melt the butter in a large non-stick frying pan over medium heat. When the butter is sizzling, remove the sandwiches from the egg mixture, allowing any excess to drip off, and place in the pan. Cook for 2 minutes on each side, or until well browned. Cut the sandwiches in half and serve immediately dusted with the icing sugar.

TIP: You can also use four slices of hand-cut cob or cottage loaf instead of the brioche, if you wish.

Chocolate hazelnut wheels

MAKES 16

100 g (3½ oz) unsalted butter, softened
55 g (2 oz/¼ cup) caster (superfine) sugar
1 egg, at room temperature
125 g (4½ oz/1 cup) plain (all-purpose) flour
30 g (1 oz/¼ cup) unsweetened cocoa powder
55 g (2 oz/½ cup) ground hazelnuts
70 g (2½ oz/½ cup) hazelnuts, toasted, skinned and chopped

Chocolate filling
100 g (3½ oz) dark chocolate (54 per cent cocoa solids), chopped
50 g (1¾ oz) butter, softened
40 g (1½ oz/⅓ cup) icing (confectioners') sugar, sifted

Beat the butter and sugar in a large bowl using electric beaters until just combined, then add the egg, beating until just combined. Sift in the flour and cocoa, add the ground hazelnuts and, using a wooden spoon, stir to form a soft dough. Shape into a flat disc, cover with plastic wrap and refrigerate for 30 minutes.

Preheat the oven to 180°C (350°F/Gas 4). Line two baking trays with baking paper.

Roll out the dough on a lightly floured work surface until 5 mm (¼ inch) thick. Chill for 30 minutes, then cut the dough into 32 rounds using a 5 cm (2 inch) cookie cutter, re-rolling the dough when necessary. Place on the prepared trays, then refrigerate for 10 minutes.

Bake, swapping the trays halfway through cooking, for 15 minutes, or until the biscuits are cooked through and aromatic. Allow to cool completely on the trays.

Meanwhile, to make the chocolate filling, place the chocolate in a heatproof bowl over a saucepan of simmering water, ensuring the bowl doesn't touch the water. Stir until the chocolate has melted. Set aside to cool to room temperature. Beat the cooled, melted chocolate and the butter using electric beaters until creamy. Add the sugar and beat until well combined.

Use the chocolate filling to sandwich the biscuits together, spreading the filling around the sides of the sandwiched biscuits. Roll the biscuit sides in the chopped hazelnuts.

Filled biscuits will keep, stored in an airtight container, for up to 5 days. Unfilled biscuits will keep, stored in an airtight container, for up to 2 weeks.

White chocolate semifreddo with blackberries in syrup

SERVES 8

170 ml (5½ fl oz/⅔ cup) milk
45 g (1¾ oz/½ cup) desiccated coconut
100 g (3½ oz) white chocolate, finely chopped
2 egg yolks
55 g (2 oz/¼ cup) caster (superfine) sugar
185 ml (6 fl oz/¾ cup) whipping cream, whipped

Blackberries in syrup
2 tablespoons caster (superfine) sugar
2 tablespoons water
300 g (10½ oz) blackberries

Line a 7.5 x 25 cm (3 x 10 inch) loaf (bar) tin with plastic wrap, allowing the plastic wrap to overhang the sides.

Place the milk and coconut in a small saucepan and bring to a simmer over medium heat. Remove from the heat, cover and cool to room temperature. Strain through a fine sieve into a small saucepan, pressing with the back of a spoon to extract as much milk as possible. Add the chocolate and stir over low heat until the chocolate has melted. Remove from the heat and set aside.

Combine the egg yolks and sugar in a heatproof bowl over a saucepan of simmering water, ensuring the bowl doesn't touch the water. Beat using electric beaters until pale and very thick. Remove from the heat and beat until cooled to room temperature. Stir in the chocolate mixture.

Use a large metal spoon or spatula to fold half the cream into the chocolate mixture. Fold in the remaining cream. Pour into the prepared tin.

Cover with the overhanging plastic wrap and freeze for 6 hours, or until frozen.

To make the blackberries in syrup, combine the sugar and water in a small saucepan and stir over low heat until the sugar dissolves. Bring to a simmer, add the blackberries and heat until warmed through. Remove from the heat.

Transfer the semifreddo to a cutting board and peel away the plastic wrap. Cut into eight slices and serve with the blackberries in syrup.

This semifreddo will keep, stored in an airtight container in the freezer, for up to 2 weeks.

Milk chocolate panna cotta with poached raisins

Combine the cream, milk and sugar in a small saucepan over medium heat and bring just to a simmer, stirring to dissolve the sugar. Remove from the heat, add the chocolate and stir until the chocolate has melted.

Place the boiling water in a small heatproof dish, sprinkle on the gelatine and whisk with a fork until the gelatine dissolves. Set aside for 1 minute, or until the liquid is clear. Add to the hot chocolate mixture and stir until combined. Strain into a jug, cover and place in the refrigerator, stirring occasionally, for 1 hour, or until cooled to room temperature.

Very lightly brush six 125 ml (4 fl oz/½ cup) dariole moulds with the oil and place on a tray. Stir the cooled chocolate mixture and divide evenly among the prepared moulds. Place in the refrigerator for 6 hours, or until lightly set.

Meanwhile, to make the poached raisins, combine the raisins, Pedro Ximenez and water in a small saucepan over low heat. Simmer gently for 5 minutes, or until reduced and syrupy and the raisins are plump.

Slide a palette knife down the side of each mould to create an air pocket, then turn out onto serving plates. Serve accompanied by the poached raisins.

These panna cottas will keep, covered, in their moulds, in the refrigerator, for up to 2 days.

MAKES 6

300 ml (10½ fl oz) cream
185 ml (6 fl oz/¾ cup) milk
2 tablespoons caster (superfine) sugar
150 g (5½ oz) milk chocolate, finely chopped
2 tablespoons boiling water
2 teaspoons powdered gelatine
canola oil, to grease

Poached raisins
125 g (4½ oz/1 cup) raisins
60 ml (2 fl oz/¼ cup) Pedro Ximenez
2 tablespoons water

Chocolate and caramel sundae waffles

SERVES 4

8 x 8 cm (3¼ inch) Belgian waffles
8 scoops vanilla bean ice cream
75 g (2¾ oz/¾ cup) pecans, lightly toasted
100 g (3½ oz) dark chocolate (70 per cent cocoa solids), roughly chopped or shaved

Caramel sauce
115 g (4 oz/½ cup) caster (superfine) sugar
2 tablespoons water
60 ml (2 fl oz/¼ cup) cream
10 g (¼ oz) butter, cubed

To make the caramel sauce, combine the sugar and water in a small saucepan and stir over low heat until the sugar dissolves. Increase the heat to medium, bring to the boil and cook, without stirring, occasionally brushing down the side of the pan with a pastry brush dipped in water, until golden. Remove immediately from the heat and allow the bubbles to subside. Add the cream and butter—being careful as it may spit—and stir until smooth. Set aside and keep warm.

Toast the waffles in a toaster or according to the packet directions until warmed through.

Place two waffles on each serving plate. Top with the ice cream and half the pecans and chocolate. Drizzle on the warm caramel sauce, sprinkle with the remaining pecans and chocolate and serve immediately.

The caramel sauce will keep, stored in an airtight container or a jar in the refrigerator, for up to 1 week. Reheat, stirring frequently, in a small saucepan over low heat until warmed through.

Steamed chocolate and prune puddings with Cognac cream

Preheat the oven to 180°C (350°F/Gas 4). Grease eight 185 ml (6 fl oz/¾ cup) ramekins. Line the bases with baking paper.

To make the Cognac cream, combine the cream, sugar and Cognac in a small bowl and stir to mix well. Cover with plastic wrap and place in the refrigerator until required.

Cream the butter and brown sugar in a medium-sized bowl using electric beaters until pale and fluffy. Add the eggs, one at a time, beating well after each addition. Sift in the flour and cocoa and fold in using a large metal spoon or spatula. Fold in the milk, then add the chocolate and prunes and stir until well combined.

Spoon the mixture into the prepared ramekins and smooth the surfaces with the back of a spoon. Cover each pudding with a piece of buttered foil, folding the edges of foil tightly around the rim, and place in an ovenproof dish. Add enough boiling water to come halfway up the side of the ramekins. Bake for 45–50 minutes, or until a skewer inserted in the centre of a pudding comes out clean. Remove from the water bath and allow the puddings to stand in the ramekins for 5 minutes, then turn out onto serving plates. Serve immediately, dusted with the icing sugar and accompanied by the Cognac cream.

These puddings will keep, stored in the ramekins and covered with plastic wrap (remove the foil first) in the refrigerator, for up to 2 days.

MAKES 8

125 g (4½ oz/½ cup) unsalted butter, softened
125 g (4½ oz/⅔ cup) soft brown sugar
3 eggs, at room temperature
125 g (4½ oz/1 cup) self-raising flour
40 g (1½ oz/⅓ cup) unsweetened cocoa powder
60 ml (2 fl oz/¼ cup) milk
125 g (4½ oz) dark chocolate (54 per cent cocoa solids), chopped
125 g (4½ oz) pitted prunes, chopped
icing (confectioners') sugar, sifted, for dusting

Cognac cream
300 ml (10½ fl oz) thick (double/heavy) cream
2 tablespoons icing (confectioners') sugar, sifted
2 tablespoons Cognac

Chocolate peanut butter cups

300 g (10½ oz) dark chocolate (54 per cent
cocoa solids), chopped
125 g (4½ oz/½ cup) smooth or crunchy
peanut butter
30 g (1 oz /¼ cup) icing (confectioners') sugar
40 g (1½ oz/¼ cup) roasted unsalted
peanuts, chopped

Place 220 g (7¾ oz) of the chocolate in a heatproof bowl over a saucepan of simmering water, ensuring the bowl doesn't touch the water. Stir until the chocolate has melted. Remove from the heat. Divide the chocolate among 20 small fluted foil cases, using a teaspoon to spread the chocolate evenly up the sides to form a thin layer. Set aside for 20 minutes, or until the chocolate has cooled slightly.

Meanwhile, place the remaining 80 g (2¾ oz) of chocolate in a heatproof bowl over a saucepan of simmering water, ensuring the bowl doesn't touch the water. Stir until the chocolate has melted. Remove from the heat. Stir in the peanut butter and sugar. Spoon the filling into a piping (icing) bag fitted with a 1 cm (½ inch) plain nozzle. Pipe the filling into the chocolate cups. Top each cup with the chopped peanuts and set aside in a cool place for 1 hour, or until the filling firms slightly.

These chocolate cups will keep, stored in an airtight container, for up to 1 week.

Chocolate
swirl nougat

MAKES 40

4 sheets rice paper
150 g (5½ oz) dark chocolate (70 per cent
cocoa solids), chopped
550 g (1 lb 4 oz/2½ cups) sugar
340 g (11¾ oz/1 cup) liquid glucose
115 g (4 oz/⅓ cup) honey
2 egg whites, at room temperature
155 g (5½ oz/1 cup) blanched almonds,
lightly toasted

Line the base and long sides of a 16 x 26 cm
(6¼ x 10½ inch) non-stick baking tin with baking
paper, allowing the paper to overhang the sides. Cover
the base of the tin with two sheets of the rice paper,
cutting to fit and overlapping slightly.

Place the chocolate in a heatproof bowl over a
saucepan of simmering water, ensuring the bowl
doesn't touch the water. Stir until the chocolate has
melted. Remove from the heat and set aside.

Combine the sugar, liquid glucose and honey in a
heavy-based saucepan over low heat and stir until the
sugar has dissolved. Increase the heat to high and
bring to the boil. Place a sugar (candy) thermometer
in the syrup and boil, without stirring, until the syrup
reaches 140°C (275°F).

Meanwhile, beat the egg whites in a large heatproof
bowl using an electric beater until stiff peaks form.

Remove the syrup from the heat and allow the
bubbles to subside. Gradually pour the syrup into the
egg whites in a thin steady stream and beat until the
mixture is very thick and glossy. Working quickly, and
using a large metal spoon or spatula, fold in the melted

chocolate and almonds until swirled. Pour into the prepared tin. Place the two remaining pieces of rice paper on top, cut to fit, and press down firmly. Stand in a cool, dry place for 6 hours, or until set.

Transfer the nougat to a cutting board and use a hot, dry, sharp knife to cut into 2 x 5 cm (¾ x 2 inch) pieces.

The nougat will keep, stored in layers separated by baking paper, in an airtight container, at room temperature for 2 weeks, or in the refrigerator for up to 4 weeks (stand at room temperature for 1 hour, still in the airtight container before serving).

TIPS: Edible rice paper is available in 15 x 23 cm (6 x 9 inches) sheets from selected food stores and delicatessens. Don't confuse it with the round or square rice paper wrappers used to make spring rolls. Toast the almonds in a preheated 180°C (350°F/Gas 4) oven for 8–10 minutes, or until lightly golden and aromatic. Allow to cool on the tray.

Chocolate, raisin and pecan scrolls

MAKES 8

450 g (1 lb) plain (all-purpose) flour, sifted
2 tablespoons caster (superfine) sugar
2 teaspoons dried yeast
½ teaspoon salt
finely grated zest of 1 lemon
185 ml (6 fl oz/¾ cup) lukewarm milk
125 g (4½ oz) unsalted butter, cubed
and softened
2 egg yolks, lightly whisked
milk, extra, for brushing
icing (confectioners') sugar, sifted, for dusting

Filling

100 g (3½ oz) dark chocolate (54 per cent cocoa
solids), chopped
90 g (3¼ oz/¾ cup) raisins
75 g (2¾ oz/¾ cup) pecans, lightly toasted
and chopped
55 g (2 oz/¼ cup) soft brown sugar
50 g (1¾ oz) unsalted butter, cubed

Combine the flour, caster sugar, yeast, salt and lemon zest in a large bowl and make a well in the centre. Add the milk, butter and egg yolks and stir with a wooden spoon to form a soft dough.

Turn the dough out onto a lightly floured work surface and knead for 5 minutes, or until smooth and elastic. Shape the dough into a ball, place in a greased medium-sized bowl and cover with plastic wrap. Set aside in a warm, draught-free place for 1½ hours, or until doubled in size.

Meanwhile, to make the filling, combine the chocolate, raisins, pecans, sugar and butter in a medium-sized bowl and stir well. Set aside.

Place eight 185 ml (6 fl oz/¾ cup) straight-sided paper cases on a baking tray.

Use your fist to knock down the dough, then knead on a lightly floured work surface for 2 minutes, or until the dough has returned to its original size. Roll out the dough to form a 25 x 46 cm (10 x 18 inch) rectangle.

With a long side closest to you, spread the filling over the dough, leaving a 5 cm (2 inch) border along the side furthest away from you. Starting with the long side closest to you, roll up the dough to enclose the filling. Cut the roll into eight 5 cm (2 inch) thick slices and place, cut side up, in the paper cases. Brush the tops with the extra milk and cover loosely with plastic wrap. Place in a warm, draught-free place for 30 minutes, or until well risen.

Preheat the oven to 190°C (375°F/Gas 5). Brush the scrolls again with a little milk and bake for 10 minutes. Reduce the oven temperature to 180°C (350°F/Gas 4) and bake for 15 minutes, or until the scrolls are golden and cooked through. Serve warm, dusted with the icing sugar.

These scrolls are best eaten the day they are made.

Chocolate soufflés

Preheat the oven to 190°C (375°F/Gas 5). Lightly grease six 185 ml (6 fl oz/¾ cup) ramekins. Use 1½ tablespoons of the sugar to coat the base and sides of the ramekins. Place the ramekins on a baking tray.

Melt the butter in a small saucepan over medium heat. Stir in the flour and cook for 1 minute, or until bubbling. Gradually whisk in the milk until smooth. Continue to cook, stirring constantly, until the mixture thickens and boils. Simmer for 1 minute.

Transfer the mixture to a large heatproof bowl, add half the remaining sugar, the egg yolks and chocolate and stir until the chocolate has melted and the custard is smooth. Cover the surface of the chocolate custard with plastic wrap and place in the refrigerator, stirring occasionally, for 30 minutes, or until cooled to room temperature.

Beat the egg whites in a medium-sized bowl using electric beaters until soft peaks form. Gradually beat in the remaining sugar. Use a large metal spoon or spatula to fold half the egg whites into the chocolate custard. Fold in the remaining egg whites until just combined.

Divide the mixture evenly among the prepared ramekins and use the back of a spoon to carefully smooth the surface. Bake for 25 minutes, or until well risen. Serve immediately, dusted with the cocoa and accompanied by a dollop of cream if desired.

SERVES 6

145 g (5¼ oz/⅔ cup) caster (superfine) sugar
30 g (1 oz) unsalted butter, cubed
2 tablespoons plain (all-purpose) flour
500 ml (17 fl oz/2 cups) milk
2 eggs, at room temperature, separated
150 g (5½ oz) dark chocolate (70 per cent cocoa solids), chopped
unsweetened cocoa powder, sifted, for dusting
cream, to serve

Index

Published in 2010 by Murdoch Books Pty Limited

Murdoch Books Australia
Pier 8/9
23 Hickson Road
Millers Point NSW 2000
Phone: +61 (0) 2 8220 2000
Fax: +61 (0) 2 8220 2558
www.murdochbooks.com.au

Murdoch Books UK Limited
Erico House, 6th Floor
93–99 Upper Richmond Road
Putney, London SW15 2TG
Phone: +44 (0) 20 8785 5995
Fax: +44 (0) 20 8785 5985
www.murdochbooks.co.uk

Publisher: Jane Lawson
Photographer: Brett Stevens
Stylist: Matt Page
Recipes by: Anneka Manning
Designer: Reuben Crossman
Project manager: Livia Caiazzo
Editor: Megan Johnston
Food editor: Chrissy Freer
Production: Kita George

Text, design and photography copyright © 2009
Murdoch Books

National Library of Australia Cataloguing-in-Publication Data
Title: Indulgence Chocolate: a fine selection of sweet treats
ISBN: 9781741965155 (hbk)
Series: Indulgence series
Notes: Includes index
Subjects: cake
Dewey Number: 641.865

A catalogue record for this book is available from the
British Library.

Colour separation by SPLITTING IMAGE.

PRINTED IN CHINA.

The Publisher and stylist would like to thank Mokum
Textiles, Waterford Wedgwood, Radford Furnishings,
No Chintz and Murobond.

IMPORTANT: Those who might be at risk from the effects of
salmonella poisoning (the elderly, pregnant women, young
children and those suffering from immune deficiency
diseases) should consult their doctor with any concerns about
eating raw eggs.

OVEN GUIDE: You may find cooking times vary depending
on the oven you are using. For fan-forced ovens, as a general
rule, set the oven temperature to 20°C (35°F) lower than
indicated in the recipe.